The Richest Man in Babylon Action Plan

T0150980

The Master Class Series

The Richest Man in Babylon Action Plan

ANCIENT WEALTH PRINCIPLES FOR TOUGH NEW TIMES

A MASTER CLASS COURSE WITH

Mitch Horowitz

Includes a bonus condensation
of the original classic

MEDIA

Published 2021 by Gildan Media LLC
aka G&D Media
www.GandDmedia.com

FIRST EDITION 2021

Cover design by Tom McKeveny

Interior design by Meghan Day Healey of Story Horse, LLC

Library of Congress Cataloging-in-Publication Data is available
upon request

ISBN: 978-1-7225-0326-0

10   9   8   7   6   5   4   3   2   1

Contents

Introduction
The Book of Gold

Truth, by its nature, does not change with the times. And the principles of George S. Clason's classic guide to financial health, *The Richest Man in Babylon*, remain as ardently useful in the 21st century as they did when he began writing his lessons in pamphlet form in 1926 and publishing them as a book four years later. Clason's core lesson to "pay yourself first"—which requires saving at least ten percent of your income before spending it on anything else—is now a standard principle in many financial guides.

Because Clason's lessons are universal, however, does not mean that they do not require updating in light of current financial challenges. I am writing these words in the midst of the worldwide Covid pandemic, now entering its second year. Our world is facing an economic crisis not dissimilar to the Great Depression, which coincided with Clason's original book. But with several key differences:

1. **Healthcare costs.** Clason wrote *The Richest Man in Babylon* in an era when medical care and health insurance operated on a different economic scale. For that reason, no mention of the spiraling cost of healthcare appears in Clason's text, nor any mention of how to fit this out-of-control expense into one's budgeting needs.

2. **Economic shutdown.** Even after our economy recovers from the Covid crisis, individuals and businesses face long-term aftereffects, changing how we work and compelling us to balance savings and debt repayment with the need for liquidity and on-hand cash.

3. **Start-up costs.** As increasing numbers of people pursue self-employment or work long-term from home, a certain degree startup costs—sometimes funded through debt—will be necessary to cover the various tech and tools of home and self-employment or entrepreneurship.

In this "action plan" I take these concerns into account while applying the insights of Clason's original lessons.

Before launching into the current-day application of Clason's principles, let me offer some background on the author and his work. Clason presented *The Richest Man in Babylon* as a series of parables from the ancient Mesopotamian empire. As alluded, the author is credited with minting the phrase and principle of "paying yourself first," which means setting aside at least ten percent of your earnings in savings and dedicating the remainder of your money to paying down debt, procuring a home or other investment properties, buying insurance, caring for your family, and only then allowing yourself to spend on life's pleasures.

Clason's approach was one of thrift. "Every piece of gold you save is a slave to work for you," one of his ancient characters says. He did not endorse asceticism; indeed he wanted money management approached in a spirit of joy and adventure—knowing that your prudence will eventually pay off in comfort and security. This is the aim of his down-to-basics lessons in prudence and safe investment. And he got rich himself offering them.

In the early twentieth century, Clason was a Denver-based publisher of maps and atlases.

He published the first road atlas of the United States and Canada. In 1926, he hit upon an idea that later saved his own finances and preserved his name as one of the most popular self-help writers of the last century, and our own. Clason began writing a series of pamphlets on managing personal finances, which banks, insurance companies, and brokerage houses bought in bulk and distributed free to their clients. The map-maker's pamphlets proved so popular that in 1930 he grouped them together in a single volume, which he issued from his own publishing company.

Clason Publishing did not survive the Great Depression. But *The Richest Man in Babylon* did—and in the years ahead it emerged as a mainstay of popular financial literature.

Clason's outlook was ardently business-friendly. Companies that sold insurance, issued mortgages, or maintained savings accounts had everything to like about it. Clason endorsed modern financial products along with a cheerful and self-sacrificing work ethic. Yet for all its institutional friendliness, Clason's book also contains solid, principled advice. There is not a fickle or unrealistic passage in it.

For me, the book's most effective section is chapter seven, "The Camel Trader of Babylon," which is about the imperative of paying down your debts, and the feelings of nobility that accrue to the individual who does so, even if incrementally. This principle reminds me of a passage that I read from The Talmud as a teen: "Who is evil?" a rabbi asks his students. After rumination, the answer comes: "He who borrows and does not repay." That statement must be understood on many levels; but one cannot neglect the material level.

Keep in mind that debts mean not only monetary borrowings, but also deadlines or obligations in any area of life where you've given your word. If you've vowed to complete a task, even a seemingly small domestic chore, or to show up at a certain time, then do so. You would be surprised how carefully people note such things, including your family. However you see yourself, you are evaluated and defined by your incremental workaday ethics. Whether you are aware, you also experience your own sense of performance and reliability internally; this can feed feelings of shame and anger, or of dignity and appropriateness.

It is, of course, natural to excuse yourself for those times when you feel justifiably late or in default on a commitment: aren't there exceptions for unforeseen circumstance? Yes; but you should always be very disciplined about such cases. As a friend once put it: "The only real emergency is a medical emergency." Consider this before you delay a debt, project, or commitment.

Clason helped clarify another principle for me: You should dedicate twice as much money to your debts as to your savings. Immediately save your ten percent, he wrote; but *twenty percent* should go toward debt. Debt is a drain both in terms of interest and reputation, which today often means credit score.

Clason also cautioned against any kind of investment, venture, or financial collaboration in businesses that are unfamiliar to you. That may sound commonsensical but I've come to believe that there's no such thing as common-sense. Notice how the term is invoked only to denote its absence. There is a *good sense*, which includes doing your homework. Odd as it may sound, I have known investors and financiers who proved indifferent to learning the basics of fields or businesses in which they sought to expand. Sometimes they were overconfident. A billionaire venture capitalist once told me: "There are lots of great ideas out there. But much rarer than great ideas is great execution. When I invest, I look for great execution" He told story after story of entrepreneurs who neglected elementary research into products from which they sought to profit. Such stories rarely have happy endings. My wish is that this action plan, combined with Clason's time-tested insights, will produce happy outcomes for you during tough times and beyond.

Before we begin let me add a brief note about structure. This action plan is organized as a series of "Clason's Golden Lessons" in which I distill, apply, and, where needed, update the author's key insights. Within these seven lessons and the aphorisms that follow, I believe you will discover fresh ways of applying enduring ideas. The action plan does not echo the dramatized storytelling of *The Richest Man in Babylon*—but you will find that feature along with Clason's full range of ideas in the bonus condensation of his original work at the end of this volume. Nothing substitutes for reading Clason's complete book, but the abridgement is a good refresher and adjunct to the 1930 edition. Within this journey, I believe you will discover the enduring power of these hallowed principles and how to apply them today.

—Mitch Horowitz
New York City
2021

Clason's Golden Lessons

Lesson
ONE

The Law of
Ten Percent

"Pay yourself first" is the foundational commandment of *The Richest Man in Babylon*.

You must set aside at least ten percent of your income into savings as soon as you're paid. If you work in a corporate job, taxes are probably already withheld. If you are a contractor or a freelancer, I advise subtracting this ten percent from the remaining *net* of your income after you have subtracted thirty percent for taxes. And never neglect withholding that thirty percent; in time, it will bring you greater peace of mind than you may imagine, whether you pay taxes quarterly or at the year's end.

This ten-percent savings can be higher but Clason recognized that the figure is unlikely to be missed from your income. It is a serious but manageable sum. (I recognize that during Covid and other crises such a sum may, in fact, be missed, or sometimes prove unmanageable; I address this in lesson five.) This practice fulfills the principle of accumulation. One of Clason's characters observes:

> Every gold piece you save is a slave to work for you. Every copper it earns is its child that also can earn for you. If you would become wealthy, then what you save must earn, and its children must earn, that all may help to give to you the abundance you crave . . . A part of all you earn is yours to keep. It should be not less than a tenth no matter how little you earn. It can be as much more as you can afford. Pay yourself first. Do not buy from the clothes-maker and the sandal-maker more than you can pay out of the rest.
>
> Wealth, like a tree, grows from a tiny seed. The first copper you save is the seed from which your tree of wealth shall grow. The sooner you plant that seed the sooner shall the tree grow. And the more faithfully you nourish and water that tree with consistent savings, the sooner may you bask in contentment beneath its shade.

No matter your obligations, Clason advises, set aside this ten percent—just as though it is a

vital, nonnegotiable expense like rent or mortgage. It is your hallowed payment to yourself,
no more to be bargained away than a monthly
bill you regard as basic to your existence. As
Clason writes, "A part of all you earn is yours
to keep."

Lesson
TWO

Control Your Expenses

One of Clason's character's makes a key observation: "All men are burdened with more desires than they can gratify." You will never find yourself in a position where you can buy whatever you want. This is true of even the very rich. I personally knew of a famous author who grew extremely wealthy writing popular thrillers. Yet he was always filled with financial dissatisfaction. He would look across the golf course in the development where he lived and see the home of a tech magnate that was larger than his. This author possessed more than most people could dream of but his psyche was burdened with a sense of lack. On a publicity tour, he even made a media escort pay for a cup of coffee that he bought from a street cart. That's not someone who enjoys wealth but who fears lack. (A special consideration of fear and money appears in lesson seven.)

The point I am trying to make is that budget-setting and acknowledging limits may seem like a dreary or depriving act; but every one of us, even the very wealthy, must make peace with some form of financial limit. No one gets to buy everything he sees or wants. Although a certain minimum of income is necessary for happiness, our desires tend to rise in tandem with our earnings.

Clason summed up this situation with two aphorisms: 1) "That which each of us calls our 'necessary expenses' will always grow equal to our incomes unless we protest to the contrary." 2) "Confuse not the necessary expenses with thy desires."

As alluded, budgeting is an act about which we all feel conflicted. We wish for the good things in life and limits always seem like having to get up from a meal without your hunger abated. But this predicament is often a matter of perspective. Here is one of Clason's most penetrating passages:

> Each of you, together with your good fami-
> lies, have more desires than your earnings
> can gratify. Therefore are thy earnings

spent to gratify these desires insofar as they will go. Still thou retainest many ungratified desires.

All men are burdened with more desires than they can gratify. Because of my wealth thinkest thou I may gratify every desire? There are limits to my time. There are limits to my strength. There are limits to the distance I may travel. There are limits to what I may eat. There are limits to the zest with which I may enjoy.

I say to you that just as weeds grow in a field wherever the farmer leaves space for their roots, even so freely do desires grow in men whenever there is a possibility of their being gratified. Thy desires are a multitude and those that thou mayest gratify are but few.

Study thoughtfully thy accustomed habits of living. Herein may be most often found certain accepted expenses that may wisely be reduced or eliminated. Let thy motto be one hundred percent of appreciated value demanded for each coin spent.

Therefore, engrave upon the clay each thing for which thou desireth to spend. Select those that are necessary and possible through the expenditure of nine-tenths of thy income. Cross out the rest and consider them but a part of that great multitude of desires that must go unsatisfied and regret them not.

Budget then thy necessary expenses. Touch not the one-tenth that is fattening thy purse. Let this be thy great desire that is being fulfilled. Remember: the purpose of a budget is to help thy purse to fatten. It is to assist thee to have thy necessities and, insofar as attainable, thy other desires. It is to enable thee to realize thy most cherished desires by defending them from thy casual wishes. Like a bright light in a dark cave thy budget shows up the leaks from thy purse and enables thee to stop them and control thy expenditures for definite and gratifying purposes.

This, then, is the second cure for a lean purse. Budget thy expenses that thou mayest have coins to pay for thy necessities, to pay for thy enjoyments, and to gratify thy worthwhile desires without spending more than nine-tenths of thy earnings.

In lesson five, which deals with paying down debt, I revisit the question of specific expenses—and which ones work for and against you.

Lesson
THREE

Make Your Money Multiply

Clason advised to "put each coin to laboring." By this he meant not just sitting on your savings but dedicating them to sound and safe investments.

In that vein, I want to share a personal story. Recent to this writing I was visiting the home of a successful financier for Thanksgiving. Many of the people seated around the table were financial analysts, investors, and denizens of Wall Street. I said the following: "I want to put a question to you financial wizards—and I want you to be completely frank with me. For more than twenty years, I have invested in nothing other than index funds—and not only have my long-term returns been outstanding but I have found that they surpass the returns I've heard about in various hedge funds managed by industry superstars. Am I have correct that over time index funds do better than virtually all structured funds?" Each one agreed.

If you work in a corporate job with access to a 401k account—especially with employer matches—I urge you max out contributing the legal limit, or work your way up to it. I did this for many years in a publishing job and it made all the difference in my financial life. A Roth IRA is also a greatly useful tool. When contributing to investment accounts, my advice, which speaks to Clason's need for sound, safe investment, is to rely on index funds, which generally rebound even following severe economic downturns. During the Covid crisis in spring of 2020 my fund lost nearly half its value. It was harrowing. But by the year's end it had more than made up all of the lost ground. I cannot promise that such rebounds will continue open-endedly but that kind of recovery has been my experience during two financial meltdowns: the mortgage crash of 2008 and the Covid lockdown of 2020 and now early 2021 as I write these words.

As noted, Clason was adamant that you must avoid investing in fields or funds of which you know little. Writing on the eve of and during the Great Depression, he had an allergy to any kind of financial speculation. I have witnessed people lose their money—as well as their emotional and ethical compass points—by venturing into seemingly exciting fields, including tech and media, without appropriate research, background, and understanding, as well as *willingness* to put in due diligence. The time to learn sailing is not when on you're the open seas but before you embark.

Lesson
FOUR

Make Your Home Pay

In terms of residence, owning versus buying is the perennial debate. Clason came down firmly on the principle of home ownership and vested equity. "Make of thy dwelling a profitable investment," he wrote.

On a related note, the mortgage crisis that triggered the Great Recession of 2008 ought to make every consumer wary of "too-good-to-be-true" credit and mortgage offers. In the years leading up to that crisis, speculators, predatory lenders, and short-sighted banking officers and loan guarantors issued millions of unsustainable mortgages, sometimes with deceptively low introductory rates, and often with complete foreknowledge that borrowers would prove unable to repay them. Predatory lenders and financial giants then bunched these poison loans into securities products to be sold, traded, and gambled on. This included gambling on their *failure*. The market literally incentivized failure and mass suffering on the part of American consumers. The resulting losses nearly toppled the nation's banking system and created waves of foreclosures, evictions, and home abandonment on a scale that I do not believe we as a nation have ever fully come to terms with emotionally, financially, legally, and ethically.

Mortgages are wonderful tools but they must be approached with care and fiscal conservatism.

I am an urban dweller who rents rather than owns. Am I breaking Clason's rule? To some degree, yes. But financial analysts are divided on the matter. The benefits of owning a home that increases in value under a thirty-year mortgage are plain and undeniable. And yet . . . some argue that housing costs are never a free ride, and that you are, under almost every circumstance, going to sustain a net outflow of expenses for the financing and maintenance of a home. Hence, renting may not be the money-suck that if first appears, especially if you're using your money and household productively in other ways. For example, during the Covid crisis many of us have worked from home. This may prove an enduring trend in years to come. As a writer, working from home has long been a part of my life. I realize that it is vital to claim appropriate tax deductions for the household space and utilities that facilitate working from home. Never neglect that.

It is also important in years ahead to watch carefully for the manner in which employers may allow, encourage—or even require—employees to work from home. Think of it: it's a great deal for employers. You're providing and upkeeping the space, often the technology, and almost always the utilities and maintenance. Indeed, we are poised for a new era in which employees effectively function as uncompensated landlords to their employers. If this continues—and on some scale it almost certainly will—new laws, protections, and tax deductions will be required to meet this shift in work life. If you're like me, you probably have little faith that legislation benefiting the wage-earning employee will arrive in any complete way; hence, it is vital to understand and exercise current tax laws that recognize the value you invest in your home-work setup.

A home now doubles as a workplace. You should benefit from both.

Lesson
FIVE

Debts Are Enemies

In a vital and often overlooked point, Clason wrote that you must dedicate *twice* the sum of your regular savings—your ten-percent minimum—to paying down debt. I set aside ten percent and endeavor to pay down debt at twenty percent. Indeed, Clason urges that you do everything you can, both financially and as a matter of personal and ethical resolve, to get debt-free. There is a dimension of psychological wellness and self-respect to reducing debt. In *The Richest Man in Babylon* one character tells another:

> Does not thy great king fight his enemies in every way he can and with every force he has? Thy debts are thy enemies. They ran thee out of Babylon. You left them alone and

they grew too strong for thee. Hadst fought them as a man, thou couldst have conquered them and been one honored among the townspeople. But thou had not the soul to fight them and behold thy pride hast gone down until thou are a slave in Syria.

The character being spoken to does return to Babylon with steely resolve to clear his name and pay down his debt at which he finally succeeds. As noted, Clason believed that a significant dimension of morale and self-respect are required to sustain the determination to pay-down debt. I have personally found this true.

I hardly need to tell you about the dangers of revolving debt on credit cards, which generally carry yearly interest rates of more than twenty percent. (Cash advances are even higher—avoid them like exposed electrical wires other than in an emergency.) The compound effects can be staggering. Billionaire Mark Cuban was once asked for his core financial advice for everyday people. Don't use credit cards, he said.

For a billionaire such advice seems plain—and I honor it. But I also know the real-world pressures that lead to debt, including high-interest credit-card debt. The fact is: at some point in life nearly all of us are going to use credit cards to purchase things we need, either medical, educational, or work-related. In such cases, you can attempt to take out a low-interest loan to consolidate and payoff debt. Some banks even offer such loans on the remaining balance of your card—*but be wary*: while these loans may carry a fixed yearly interest rate as low as 8.99 percent (less than half your average credit-card rate) they often come with a high monthly repayment schedule. Taking them on is the equivalent of a D-Day assault on your debt. Be ready for it.

Credit cards or any kind of loans are poison when used to purchase luxuries. A word of advice: always buy or lease a car one step below the class that you afford. A lawyer told me that he knows a client is responsible when he or she drives a car below their tax bracket; that, he said, is an infallible indicator of financial responsibility.

In terms of personal accoutrements, it is far better to pay cash for one or two quality items, such as a Schott leather jacket or Chanel skirt, than a closetful of so-so items purchased on credit. A friend who studied fashion in Paris told me that one of her teachers would come to class each day wearing the same black Chanel skirt. At first, she thought it was weird. Then she realized the teacher was exemplifying a principle. In Rome, the best cabdrivers wear designer suits. In many cases, it is the only suit they own. They always look great.

Fashion or consumer items aside, I want to revisit the question: what are appropriate or necessary expenses? In that area I am guided by the 1860 essay "Wealth" by Ralph Waldo Emerson. The Transcendentalist philosopher declares, chin out, that the individual is "born to be rich." And by riches, Emerson means cold, hard cash. But he also identifies accumulation of capital as befitting only that person who uses it to *productive ends*. Emerson writes:

> Every man is a consumer, and ought to be a producer. He fails to make his place good in the world, unless he not only pays his debt, but also adds something to the common wealth. Nor can he do justice to his genius, without making some larger demand on the world than a bare subsistence. He is by constitution expensive, and needs to be rich.

Emerson concludes that *only those purchases that expand your power and abilities* leave you any richer. Indeed, wealth that fails to accompany expansion is wealth thrown away. "Nor is the man enriched," he writes, "in repeating the old experiments of animal sensation." Rather, you are enriched when you increase your ability to earn, to do, and to grow. When you are contemplating a purchase outside of basic needs ask: Is there a *circuitry of return* on this item or am I just spending money on sensation? Wealth, properly understood, is power—and power must be renewable. Bear that in mind whenever you part with any your resources, including your time.

In sum, Emerson's advice is *to spend in ways that increase your capacity to earn*. In today's terms, that might mean investing in technology, training, and tools of your profession, art, or trade. "The man who seeks to learn more of his craft shall be richly rewarded," Clason writes. Seen in that light, anything that *enhances your abilities* is a worthy expense and, to me, a legitimate reason to take on debt if properly managed and monitored.

Given that I am writing these words during the Covid pandemic, which is shaking the finances of nearly every household, I must add a special caveat. During periods of financial crisis it is vital to maintain *liquidity*. You must have cash on hand. In such cases, it is advisable to cease paying down debt (other than managing legally minimum payments) in order to sustain your cash access. Depending on the interest rate of your debt, you may instead opt to suspend your ten-percent savings—yet the ten-percent set aside can be used for on-hand cash whereas debt repayment does not necessarily translate to liquidity. In all realism, it is sometimes necessary to break a rule in order to remain solvent during periods of crisis. Break or suspend a rule only during periods of true urgency.

Finally, I must say word about a source of debt that Clason did not address and that was not the same issue in his era that it is in ours: medical costs and healthcare insurance. Healthcare, prescriptions, and health insurance present a grave financial difficulty, and often impossibility, for millions of Americans. Political reforms may eventually control pharmaceutical prices, create a public option, expanded Medicare, or some other form of affordable insurance (universal basic income, or UBI, coupled with price controls may accomplish this, too), and protect consumers dealing with recalcitrant and misleading insurance companies. The last of these problems could be helped by transparency laws that regulate and shine daylight on arcane coding schemes insurers use to deny or delay coverage. Until reform arrives, or if it ever does, my operative principle is that most health insurance in America today is organized crime with a refrigerator magnet. Hence, their "services"—which are based on a model of taking in as high a premium as possible and paying out as few claims as possible—must be approached with prudential thought and caution.

If you work in a corporate or union job and receive good health insurance you are fortunate. Yet even those plans have gaps and lock you into a group model where you have very little consumer choice. If you are an independent worker, service worker, or contractor, the options become thinner and more stressful. Most personal finance writers ignore or gloss over this reality in their programs to wealth and solvency.

For example, starting in 2015 (and continuing through 2020) financial journalists fell in love with writing about a Vermont janitor who died with $8 million in the bank, which he left to his local library and hospital. It sounds like a great American parable: the "millionaire next door" makes good through savings and thrift, and it's all the more touching that the self-made philanthropist was a laborer. But the news coverage omitted one crucial fact. The man served in World War II—and there's the answer: *he had lifelong healthcare through the Veterans Administration*. That's what made it all possible. I know a cat sitter in Manhattan who has amassed a huge portfolio through his Roth IRA. He's a wonderful eccentric who lives cheaply in a rent-controlled apartment, eschews digital culture, cable, cell service, eating out, and most luxuries. He exists like an urban Thoreau. Like the janitor, he's also a millionaire. And like his counterpart, he is a veteran, in this case from Vietnam. He receives lifelong VA coverage, which got him through a harrowing illness.

If these thrifty men didn't have VA coverage, all of the money that they wisely invested would've been wiped out by a single health emergency, chronic condition, or purchasing of their own insurance. It is that simple. Few people who write on investment strategies or personal finance get it. We need more working people in financial journalism who know what it means to purchase insurance or otherwise cover health costs without a corporate or family net.

For freelancers and contractors, I wish I had a magic bullet to offer, but I do not. If you have children then you need insurance; it's that simple. Some states help close that gap. If you're single, look carefully at the question of health insurance. Most of the Affordable Care Act, or Obamacare, plans that are anywhere near affordable are limited in coverage, do not include prescriptions, and come with high deductibles. You might consider whether they are worth it at all. I wish there existed catastrophic-care plans that really held down costs and allowed you to plan for emergencies, but those are difficult to find especially if you're over 40.

All I am really trying to say is: if you are independently employed do careful research (including into healthcare savings accounts), consider whether or what coverage makes sense for you, and think flexibly about your needs.

Lesson
SIX

Increase Your Ability to Earn

In late 2020, I was touched by the candor of a therapist on Twitter who tweeted: "As a therapist I can say confidently, that while therapy is helpful, what most people really need is money." Given that the number of retweets exceeded 100,000, her honesty clearly resonated with a lot of people. There were also vocal critics. I personally considered her statement an important acknowledgment.

Clason, too, noted that sometimes—in fact, often—people simply need more money. I see three steps in his outlook on how to earn more. They are simple. But look twice at them. It is only when you apply or live with a seemingly simple idea that its greater dimensions become clear. That is why cynics rarely get at the truth of things. They see simplicity as naïveté. Simplicity is the language of truth.

Here are Clauson's three steps:

1. You must sincerely and powerfully desire to earn more. Doesn't everyone? Well, not exactly. This does not mean an unspecified wish to "get rich." Or a "sure, why not?" attitude. It means a burning and specific desire to increase your earning ability. And be specific: how much do you want to earn and how? Don't vacillate. Name an amount. For help in this area, I recommend reading Napoleon Hill's *Think and Grow Rich*. If you've already read it, read it again. I reread it once a year. I often advise readers to do its exercises as though their lives depend on it. If you do, things will change for the better.

2. **One victory naturally leads to another.** What you do on a micro scale can be repeated on a macro scale. "As above, so below," goes the Hermetic dictum. One act of earning extra money teaches you your capability and generally leads to more. Don't overshoot and get disappointed. Be focused, clear, and active.

When you succeed you will have discovered a stepping stone.

3. **Cultivate skill and excellence.** This principle encompasses many things. You must not only do a job well and expeditiously, but you must keep up with the technology of your field. This is not always easy for me. I am tech-shy. But I impel myself to stay current. When I fall behind, I strive to make up for it. Another thing that cultivates excellence is sobriety. Like many people, I enjoy booze and other intoxicants. But they can disrupt sleep patterns, foster lethargy, and contribute to negative or obsessive thoughts. Even if temporarily, stop drinking or using recreational drugs when you want to earn more. It's a real help and its entirely in your hands. In 2018, conservative commentator Tucker Carlson made this simple—again watch for that word—observation: "Choices do matter, for sure. I quit drinking so I could be more successful—and it worked." Here is a further ingredient to excellence and reputation: pay your debts quickly, especially to contractors and freelancers. Such an act fosters comity and loyalty. Those people depend on your timely

payment as you do on your weekly paycheck. Pay them quickly and they become dedicated allies in your efforts.

In further probing how to earn more money, I want to return to Emerson's neglected classic "Wealth." The philosopher outlined roughly three steps to accumulating money: 1) First filling some nonnegotiable, subsistence-level need in your own life: this is what drove the primeval farmers, hunter-gathers, and villagers. 2) Next, applying one's particular talents to nature, and expansively filling the needs of others. If you do not know or understand your talents, you must start there before anything is possible. Your particular talent is a source of excellence. And, finally, 3) using your wealth for the purposes of productiveness: paying down debts, making compound investments, and procuring the tools and training of your trade. Building and expanding are the only sound ways to amass money. And such efforts reflect your code and fiber as a progressing being.

Also, when offered opportunities to earn, act decisively. Do not dither. I was once offered a massive book contract for which I felt unprepared. I quickly caught myself and said yes. It was one of the best decisions my life. Growing up, my mother told me never to refuse business. That was sound advice. I am absolutely shocked when I see storeowners, managers, or contractors turn away business. Actually turn away people who want to pay them for a service and who need their service. I saw this occur even during the Covid recession. In Brooklyn, New York, where I live, I witnessed computer and bicycle stores turn away customers—or shun them by requiring weeks-long waits—rather than expand, hire new people (a greatly productive thing to do for your community, especially during a recession), and embrace new business. To me, refusing work is one of the most deleterious of practices. There is always an excuse to say no. Rarely a good one. Do not be that person.

The cultivation of excellence and purpose is so important, and was to Clason, that I want to return to the question from a different angle. In 1854 the pioneering scientist and germ theorist Louis Pasteur said in a lecture: "In the fields of observation chance favors only the prepared mind." This statement has been popularly—and, I think, accurately—shortened into: "Chance favors the prepared mind." If you want to foster earning opportunities in your life, make it your motto.

Chance opportunities are useful only to those who are prepared for them—and the greater the preparation the more fully you will be able to take advantage of them when they arrive. Preparation means training, studying, reliability, keeping your word, and showing up ready to perform whatever task you face. It heightens all of the other chance factors around you; it ensures that you'll be in the right mental state to notice, receive, and profit from opportunities. That's why I don't believe in opportunities just coming "out of the blue." Opportunities require context.

The motivational writer Dale Carnegie began his career in the early twentieth century as a teacher of public speaking. A former actor, Carnegie grasped that public speaking was becoming a vital business skill in the years following World War I. When preparing for a talk or pitch, Carnegie advised that you should amass so much material that you discard ninety-percent of it when actually speaking. The very fact of your preparation gives you the confidence and power to speak without notes, and to deliver a relaxing, enthusiastic, and freestyle performance.

Carnegie's formula is a recipe for good outcomes in every area of life. Once you are justifiably confident and expert in a task or project, you can watch, listen, intuit, and become cognizant of important cues. Ardent preparation makes you persuasive. Your actions are natural and effortless. You can pivot. You exude confidence. You gain a childlike exuberance.

When opportunities appear before you, such as a job opening, an audition, a call to present on the fly at a conference, or even being seated next to your boss or a senior manager on an air flight (I'm waxing optimistic about a post-Covid world), the prepared person will be able to seize that golden moment. Always remember: *Luck favors the prepared mind.*

Lesson
SEVEN

Do Not Be Conquered By Fear

Clason addresses the topic of money and fear only indirectly. But I think the role of fear in personal finance requires amplification and exploration. The fact is, many of us grew up with—and are controlled by—fearful attitudes around money. This is natural. No human quality other than sexuality is fraught with greater or more complex emotions than money. That is why we are often prone to irrational actions around money, including massive debt spending or the breaking of family ties and friendships over financial disputes.

Emotion rules money. That is a core truth of life. As such, fear often controls us in areas of money management, earnings, debt, and a sense of financial security. This can cloud our decision-making and spoil our enthusiasm for life. I write these words from experience. I grew up in a childhood home devastated by financial crisis and it marked me ever after.

Yet in adulthood I also came to realize that fear—unless calling attention to a legitimate need for safety at times of crisis—rarely produces sound judgment or responses relating to money or anything else. In actuality, fear is the greatest barrier to your personal progress and capacity for action. Procrastination itself is a type of fear and is probably the most common (and overlooked) form that fear takes. Note this carefully in connection with the previous lesson on self-development.

As you begin any new undertaking you, at one point are another, likely to find yourself palpably gripped by fear. Depending on your nature, you may experience this constantly, or at least more often than you would like. You may also experience the paralysis of fear when confronting financial decisions or problems. At a certain point nearly everyone does. My wish is that you use crisis as a goad to action. "Opposition is true Friendship," wrote poet William Blake. We grow only when challenged. But we cannot grow if fear dominates us.

In that vein, I am providing a condensation of Napoleon Hill's immensely important advice on fear from his 1937 *Think and Grow*

Rich, which I referenced previously. Whenever you feel plagued by fear, including in the middle of the night or the early hours of the morning when you should be sleeping, I want you to reflect on this short passage. (There may be times I'm doing it with you.) It is the absolute truth. Let it serve as a beacon to guide you through the corridors of fear. If you find this passage useful, write it down, hang it up someplace you can see it—and share it.

> Fear should never be bargained with or capitulated to. It takes the appeal from your personality, destroys the possibility of accurate thinking, diverts concentration of effort, stifles persistence, turns your willpower into nothingness, erases ambition, clouds your memory, and invites failure in every conceivable form.
>
> Fear kills love, assassinates the finer emotions of the heart, discourages friendship, and leads to sleeplessness, misery, and unhappiness.
>
> So pernicious and destructive is the emotion of fear that it is, almost literally, worse than anything that can befall you.
>
> If you suffer from a fear of poverty, reach a decision to get along with whatever wealth you can accumulate WITHOUT WORRY. If you fear the loss of love, reach a decision to

get along without love, if that becomes necessary. If you experience a general sense of worry, reach a blanket decision that *nothing that life has to offer is worth the price of fear.* This places Ultimate Truth at your back.

And remember: The greatest of all remedies for fear is a BURNING DESIRE FOR ACHIEVEMENT, backed by useful action in pursuit of your aim.

Clason's Golden Aphorisms

The following is a collection of useful aphorisms and insights from *The Richest Man In Babylon*. Each is a lesson in itself.

Truth is always simple.

*There is no chain of disasters
that will not come to an end.*

*Where the determination is,
the way can be found.*

Thy debts are thine enemies.

*Paying debt surpasses savings.
One-tenth to savings; two-tenths to debt;
seven-tenths to home and family.*

*Money is the medium through which
earthly success is measured.*

*It costs nothing to ask wise advice
from a good friend.*

*Wealth is power. With wealth
many things are possible.*

*Every gold piece you save
is a slave to work for you.*

*Opportunity is a haughty goddess
who wastes no time with those
who are unprepared.*

*Willpower is but the unflinching
purpose to carry a task you set
for yourself to fulfillment.*

*Wealth grows wherever
men exert energy.*

*Seek the advice of men whose
daily work is handling money.*

*A small return and a safe one is
far more desirable than risk.*

That which each of us calls "necessary expenses" will always grow equal to our incomes unless we protest to the contrary.

Confuse not the necessary expenses with thy desires.

All men are burdened with more desires than they can gratify.

The purpose of a budget is to help thy purse fatten.

Study carefully, before parting with thy treasure, each assurance that it may be safely reclaimed.

Desires must be simple and definite. They defeat their own purpose should they be too many, too confusing or beyond a man's training to accomplish.

The man who seeks to learn more of his craft shall be richly rewarded.

Cultivate thy own powers . . . study and become wiser, to become more skillful, to so act as to respect thyself.

*Delay not! . . . good luck waits to come
to the man who accepts opportunity.*

*We mortals are changeable.
Alas, I must say more apt to change
our minds when right than wrong.*

*Good luck can be enticed
by accepting opportunity.*

*If you desire to help thy friend do so
in a way that will not bring thy friend's
burdens upon thyself.*

Better a little caution than a great regret.

Bonus

The Richest Man In Babylon

Condensation

by George S. Clason

Abridged by Mitch Horowitz

What follows is a bonus abridgement of George S. Clason's original book from 1930. Although nothing can replace the experience of reading the full edition of *The Richest Man In Babylon*, this condensation faithfully digests the author's full range of ideas and retains the dramatization and storytelling of his original.

—MH

Author's Foreword
For Those Who Want Money

Our prosperity as a nation depends upon the personal financial prosperity of each of us as individuals.

This book deals with the personal successes of each of us. Success means accomplishments as the result of our own efforts and abilities. Proper preparation is the key to our success. Our acts can be no wiser than our thoughts. Our thinking can be no wiser than our understanding.

This book of cures for lean purses has been termed a guide to financial understanding. That, indeed, is its purpose: to offer those who are ambitious for financial success insight that will help them acquire money, keep money, and make their surpluses earn more money.

In the pages which follow, we are taken back to Babylon, the cradle in which was nurtured the basic principles of finance now recognized and used the world over.

Babylon became the wealthiest city of the ancient world because its citizens were the richest people of their time. They appreciated the value of money. They practiced sound financial principles in acquiring money, keeping money, and making their money earn more money. They provided for themselves what we all desire: incomes for the future.

—George S. Clason

Chapter One
The Man Who Desired Gold

Bansir, the chariot builder of Babylon, was thoroughly discouraged. From his seat upon the low wall surrounding his property he gazed sadly at his simple home and the open workshop in which stood a partially completed chariot.

His wife frequently appeared at the open door. Her furtive glances in his direction reminded him that the meal bag was almost empty, and he should be at work finishing the chariot.

Nevertheless, his fat, muscular body sat stolidly upon the wall. His slow mind was struggling with a problem for which he could find no answer.

Bansir was shaken from his brooding by the twanging of the strings from a familiar lyre. He turned and looked into the sensitive, smiling face of his best friend—Kobbi, the musician.

"May the gods bless thee, my good friend," began Kobbi with an elaborate salute. "Pray, from thy purse which must be bulging else thou wouldst be busy in yon shop, extract but two humble shekels and lend them to me."

"If I did have two shekels," Bansir responded, "to no one could I lend them—not even to you, my best of friends; for they would be my fortune—my entire fortune."

"What!" exclaimed Kobbi. "Thou hast not one shekel in thy purse? Have the gods brought to thee troubles?"

"A torment from the gods it must be," Bansir said. "Let us talk it over together, for we ride in the same boat. We have earned much coin in the years that have passed, yet to know the joys that come from wealth, we are left to dream about them. Are we more than dumb sheep? We live in the richest city in all the world, but we have naught."

"Never in all our years of our friendship didst thou talk like this before, Bansir." Kobbi was puzzled.

"My heart is sad," the chariot maker replied. "I wish to be a man of means. What is the matter with us? Again I ask you! Why cannot we have our just share of the good things so plentiful for those who have gold?"

"Might we not find out how others acquire gold and do as they do?" Kobbi asked.

"Perhaps there is some secret we might learn if we but sought from those who knew," replied Bansir.

"This very day," said Kobbi, "I did pass our old friend, Arkad, riding in his golden chariot. So rich is he that the king himself is said to seek his aid in affairs of the treasury."

"So rich," Bansir said, "that I fear if I should meet him in the darkness of the night I should lay my hands upon his fat wallet."

"Nonsense," reproved Kobbi, "a man's wealth is not in the purse he carries. A fat purse quickly empties if there be no golden stream to refill it. Arkad has an income that constantly keeps his purse full, no matter how liberally he spends."

"Kobbi, thou bringest to me a rare thought." A new light gleamed in Bansir's eyes. "It costs nothing to ask wise advice from a good friend, and Arkad was always that. We are weary of being without gold in the midst of plenty. Come, let us go to him and ask how we, also, may acquire incomes for ourselves."

"Thou speakest with true inspiration, Bansir. Thou bringeth to my mind a new understanding. Thou makest me to realize why we have never found any measure of wealth. We never sought it. Thou hast labored patiently to build the staunchest chariots in Babylon. To that purpose was devoted your best endeavors. Therefore, at it thou didst succeed. I strove to become a skillful lyre player. And, at it I did succeed.

"In those things toward which we exerted our best endeavors we succeeded. The gods were content to let us continue thus. Now, at last, we see a new light. It biddeth us to learn more that we may prosper more. With new understanding we shall find honorable ways to accomplish our desires."

Chapter Two
The Richest Man in Babylon

In old Babylon there once lived a certain very rich man named Arkad. Far and wide he was famed for his great wealth. He was generous in his charities. He was generous with his family. He was liberal in his own expenses. But nevertheless each year his wealth increased more rapidly than he spent it.

Certain friends of younger days came to him and said: "You are more fortunate than we. You have become the richest man in all Babylon while we struggle for existence. Yet, once we were equal. We studied under the same master. We played in the same games. And in neither the studies nor the games did you outshine us. And in the years since, you have been no more an honorable citizen than we. Nor have you worked harder or more faithfully. Why, then, should a fickle fate single you out to enjoy all the good things of life and ignore us who are equally deserving?"

Thereupon Arkad remonstrated with them, saying, "If you have not acquired more than a bare existence in the years since we were youths, it is because you either have failed to learn the laws that govern the building of wealth, or else you do not observe them.

"In my youth," the rich man continued, "I looked about me and saw all the good things there were to bring happiness and contentment. And I realized that wealth increased the potency of all these.

"And, when I realized all this, I decided that I would claim my share of the good things of life.

"Being, as you know, the son of a humble merchant, one of a large family with no hope of an inheritance, and not being endowed, as you have so frankly said, with superior powers or wisdom, I decided that if I were to achieve what I desired, time and study would be required.

"As for time, all men have it in abundance. You, each of you, have let slip by sufficient time to have made yourselves wealthy.

"As for study, did not our wise teacher teach us that learning was of two kinds: the one kind being the things we learned and knew, and the other being the training that taught us how to find out what we did not know?

"Therefore did I decide to find out how one might accumulate wealth, and when I had found out, to make this my task.

"I found employment as a scribe in the hall of records, and long hours each day I labored upon the clay tablets. Week after week, and month after month, I labored, yet for my earnings I had naught to show.

"And one day Algamish, the moneylender, came to the house of the city master and ordered a copy of the Ninth Law, and he said to me, 'I must have this in two days.'

"I labored hard, but the law was long, and when Algamish returned the task was unfinished. He was angry, and had I been his slave, he would have beaten me. But knowing that the city master would not permit him to injure me, I was unafraid, so I said to him, 'Algamish, you are a very rich man. Tell me how I may also become rich, and all night I will carve upon the clay, and when the sun rises it shall be completed.'

"He smiled and replied, 'You are a forward knave, but we will call it a bargain.'

"All that night I carved, though my back pained and the smell of the wick made my head ache until my eyes could hardly see. But when he returned at sunup, the tablets were complete.

"'You have fulfilled your part of our bargain, my son,' he said to me. 'And I am ready to fulfill mine. Mark you well my words, for if you do not you will fail to grasp the truth that I will tell you, and you will think that your night's work has been in vain.'

"Then he looked at me shrewdly and said in a low, forceful tone: 'I found the road to wealth when I decided that a part of all I earned was mine to keep. And so will you.'

"Then he continued to look at me with a glance that I could feel pierce me but said no more. 'Is that all?' I asked.

"'That was sufficient to change the heart of a sheep herder into the heart of a moneylender,' he replied.

"But all I earn is mine to keep, is it not?" I asked.

"'Far from it,' he replied. 'Do you not pay the garment-maker? Do you not pay the sandal-maker? Do you not pay for the things you eat? Can you live in Babylon without spending? What have you to show for your earnings of the past month? What for the past year? Fool! You pay to everyone but yourself. You labor for others. As well be a slave and work for what your master gives you. If you did keep for yourself one-tenth of all you earn, how much would you have in ten years?'"

"My knowledge of the numbers did not forsake me, and I answered, 'As much as I earn in one year.'

"'You speak but half the truth' he retorted. 'Every gold piece you save is a slave to work for you. Every copper it earns is its child that also can earn for you. If you would become wealthy, then what you save must earn, and its children must earn, that all may help to give to you the abundance you crave.

"'You think I cheat you for your long night's work,' he continued, 'but I am paying you a thousand times over if you have the intelligence to grasp the truth I offer.

"'A part of all you earn is yours to keep. It should be not less than a tenth no matter how little you earn. It can be as much more as you can afford. Pay yourself first. Do not buy from the clothes-maker and the sandal-maker more than you can pay out of the rest.

"'Wealth, like a tree, grows from a tiny seed. The first copper you save is the seed from which your tree of wealth shall grow. The sooner you plant that seed the sooner shall the tree grow. And the more faithfully you nourish and water that tree with consistent savings, the sooner may you bask in contentment beneath its shade.'

"So saying, he took his tablets and went away.

"I thought much about what he had said to me, and it seemed reasonable. So I decided to try it. Each time I was paid I took one from each ten pieces of copper and hid it away. And strange as it may seem, I was no shorter of funds than before.

"A twelfth month later Algamish returned and asked me, 'Son, have you paid to yourself not less than one-tenth of all you have earned for the past year?'

"I answered proudly: 'Yes, master, I have.'

"'That is good," he answered, 'and what have you done with it?'

"I have given it to Azmur, the brick maker, who told me he was travelling over the far seas and he would buy for me the rare jewels of the Phoenicians. When he returns we shall sell these at high prices.

"'Every fool must learn,' he said. 'Why trust the knowledge of a brick maker about jewels? Would you go to the bread maker to inquire about the stars? No, you would go to the astrologer, if you had power to think. Your savings are gone, youth; you have pulled your wealth-tree up by the roots. But plant another. Try again. And next time if you would have advice about jewels, go to the jewel merchant. Advice is one thing that is freely given away but watch that you take only what is worth having. He who takes advice about his savings from one who is inexperienced in such matters shall pay with his savings for proving the falsity of their opinions.' Saying this, he went away.

"And it was as he said. For the Phoenicians sold to Azmur worthless bits of glass. But as Algamish had bid me, I again saved each tenth copper, for I now had formed the habit and it was no longer difficult.

"Again, twelve months later, Algamish came and asked, 'What progress have you made since last I saw you?'

"'I have paid myself faithfully,' I replied, 'and my savings I have entrusted to Aggar the shield maker, to buy bronze, and each fourth month he does pay me the rental.'

"'That is good. And what do you do with the rental?'

"I have a great feast. Also I have bought me a scarlet tunic. And some day I shall buy me a young ass upon which to ride.

"To which Algamish replied, 'You eat the children of your savings. How do you expect them to work for you? And how can they have children that will also work for you? First get thee an army of golden slaves and then many a rich banquet may you enjoy without regret.' So saying he again went away.

"Nor did I again see him for two years. And he said to me, 'Arkad, hast thou yet achieved the wealth thou dreamed of?'

"And I answered, 'Not yet all that I desire, but some I have and it earns more, and its earnings earn more.'

"'And do you still take the advice of brick makers?'

"'About brick making they give good advice,' I said.

"'Arkad,' he continued, 'you have learned well. You first learned to live upon less than you could earn. Next you learned to seek advice from those who were competent through their own experience to give it. And, lastly, you have learned to make gold work for you. You have taught yourself how to acquire money, how to keep it, and how to use it. Therefore, you are competent for a responsible position. I am becoming an old man. My sons think only of spending and give no thought to earning. My interests are great and too much for me to look after. If you will go to Nippur and look after my lands there, I shall make you my partner and you shall share in my estate.'

"So I went to Nippur and took charge of his holdings, which were large. And because I was full of ambition and had mastered the three laws of handling wealth, I was enabled to increase greatly the value of his properties. So I prospered much, and when the spirit of Algamish departed, I did share in his estate as he had arranged under the law."

So spake Arkad, and when he had finished his tale, one of his friends said, "You were indeed fortunate that Algamish made of you an heir."

"Fortunate only in that I had the desire to prosper before I first met him. For four years did I not prove my definiteness of purpose by keeping one-tenth of all I earned? Opportunity is a haughty goddess who wastes no time with those who are unprepared."

"You had strong willpower to keep on after you lost your first year's savings," said another.

"Willpower!" retorted Arkad. "What nonsense. Do you think willpower gives a man the strength to lift a burden the camel cannot carry, or to draw a load the oxen cannot budge? Willpower is but the unflinching purpose to fulfill a task you set for yourself. Therefore, I am careful not to start difficult and impractical tasks, because I love leisure."

And then another friend spoke up and said, "If what you tell is true, then being so simple, if all men did it, would there be enough wealth to go around?"

"Wealth grows wherever men exert energy," Arkad replied. "No man can prophesy the limit of it. Have not the Phoenicians built great cities on barren coasts with the wealth that comes from their ships of commerce on the seas?"

"What then do you advise us to do that we also may become rich?" asked one of his friends.

"I advise that you take the wisdom of Algamish and say to yourselves, 'A part of all I earn is mine to keep.' Say it in the morning when you first arise. Say it at noon. Say it at night. Say it each hour of every day. Say it to yourself until the words stand out like letters of fire across the sky. Then take whatever portion seems wise. Let it be not less than one-tenth and lay it by. Arrange your other expenditures to do this if necessary.

"Soon you will realize what a rich feeling it is to own a treasure upon which you alone have claim. As it grows it will stimulate you. A new joy of life will thrill you. Greater efforts will come to you to earn more.

"Then learn to make your treasure work for you. Make it your slave. Make its children and its children's children work for you.

"Insure an income for thy future. Look thou at the aged and forget not that in the days to come you too will be numbered among them. Therefore invest thy treasure with greatest caution.

"Provide also that thy family may not want should the gods call thee to their realms. For such protection, it is always possible to make provision with small payments at regular intervals. Therefore the provident man delays not in expectation of a large sum becoming available for such a wise purpose.

"Counsel with wise men. Seek the advice of men whose daily work is handling money. A small return and a safe one is far more desirable than risk.

"Enjoy life while you are here. Do not overstrain or try to save too much. If one-tenth of all you earn is as much as you can comfortably keep, be content to keep this portion. Live otherwise according to your income; let not yourself get stingy and afraid to spend. Life is good and rich with things worthwhile and things to enjoy."

His friends thanked him and went away. In the following years, they frequently revisited Arkad, who received them gladly. He counseled them and gave freely of his wisdom, as men of broad experience are always glad to do. He assisted them in investing their savings to bring good interest with safety, and not be lost or entangled in investments that paid no dividends.

The turning point in these men's lives came upon the day when they realized the truth that had come to them:

A PART OF ALL YOU EARN IS YOURS TO KEEP

Chapter Three
Seven Cures for a Lean Purse

The glory of Babylon endures. Down through the ages its reputation comes to us as the richest of cities. Yet it was not always so. The riches of Babylon were the results of the wisdom of its people. They first had to learn how to become wealthy.

When the good king, Sargon, returned to Babylon after defeating his enemies, he

was confronted with a serious situation. The Royal Chancellor explained it to the king: "After many years of great prosperity brought to our people because your majesty built the great irrigation canals, now that these works are completed the people seem unable to support themselves. The laborers are without employment. The merchants have few customers. The farmers are unable to sell their produce. The people have not enough gold to buy food."

"But where has all the gold gone that we spent for these great improvements?" asked the king.

"It has found its way, I fear," responded the Chancellor, "into the possession of a few very rich men."

The king was thoughtful for some time. Then he asked, "Why should so few men be able to acquire all the gold?"

"Because they know how," replied the Chancellor.

The king decided that the ways of wealth must be taught to the people—and the next day he summoned to the palace Arkad, the richest man in Babylon.

"Arkad," said the king, "I desire that Babylon be the wealthiest city in the world. Therefore, it must be a city of many wealthy men. Hence, we must teach all the people how to acquire riches. Tell me, Arkad, is there any secret to acquiring wealth? Can it be taught?"

"It is practical, your majesty. That which one man knows can be taught to others. Let your chancellor arrange for me a class of one hundred men and I will teach to them the seven cures that did fatten my purse."

A fortnight later, the chosen hundred assembled in the Temple of Learning.

"As a dutiful subject of our king," Arkad began, "I stand before you in his service. Because once I was a poor youth who did greatly desire gold, and because I found knowledge that enabled me to acquire it, he asks that I impart unto you my knowledge.

"The first storehouse of my treasure was a well-worn purse. I loathed its useless emptiness. I desired that it be round and full, clinking with the sound of gold. Therefore, I sought every remedy for a lean purse. I found seven. We shall now consider each."

THE FIRST CURE

Start thy purse to fattening

"Now I shall tell thee the first remedy I learned to cure a lean purse. For every ten coins thou placest within thy purse take out for use but nine. Thy purse will start to fatten at once and its increasing weight will feel good in thy hand and bring satisfaction to thy soul.

"Deride not what I say because of its simplicity. Truth is always simple. I told thee I would tell how I built my fortune. This was my beginning. I, too, carried a lean purse and cursed it because there was naught within to satisfy my desires. But when I began to take out from my purse but nine parts of ten I put in, it began to fatten. So will thine.

"Now I will tell a strange truth, the reason for which I know not. When I ceased to pay out more than nine-tenths of my earnings, I managed to get along just as well. I was not shorter than before. Also, ere long, did coins come to me more easily than before. Surely it is a law of the gods that unto him who keepeth and spendeth not a certain part of all his earnings, shall gold come more easily. Likewise, him whose purse is empty does gold avoid.

"Which desirest thou the most? Is it the gratification of thy desires of each day, a jewel, a bit of finery, better raiment, more food; things quickly gone and forgotten? Or is it substantial belongings, gold, lands, herds, merchandise, income-bringing investments? The coins thou takest from thy purse bring the first."

"The coins thou leavest within it will bring the latter. This, my students, was the first cure I did discover for my lean purse: 'For each ten coins I put in, to spend but nine.'"

THE SECOND CURE
Control thy expenditures

"Confuse not the necessary expenses with thy desires. Each of you, together with your good families, have more desires than your earnings can gratify. Therefore are thy earnings spent to gratify these desires insofar as they will go. Still thou retainest many ungratified desires.

"All men are burdened with more desires than they can gratify. Because of my wealth thinkest thou I may gratify every desire? There are limits to my time. There are limits to my strength. There are limits to the distance I may travel. There are limits to what I may eat. There are limits to the zest with which I may enjoy.

"I say to you that just as weeds grow in a field wherever the farmer leaves space for their roots, even so freely do desires grow in men whenever there is a possibility of their being gratified. Thy desires are a multitude and those that thou mayest gratify are but few.

"Study thoughtfully thy accustomed habits of living. Herein may be most often found certain accepted expenses that may wisely be reduced or eliminated. Let thy motto be one hundred percent of appreciated value demanded for each coin spent.

"Therefore, engrave upon the clay each thing for which thou desireth to spend. Select those that are necessary and possible through the expenditure of nine-tenths of thy income. Cross out the rest and consider them but a part of that great multitude of desires that must go unsatisfied and regret them not.

"Budget then thy necessary expenses. Touch not the one-tenth that is fattening thy purse. Let this be thy great desire that is being fulfilled. Remember: the purpose of a budget is to help thy purse to fatten. It is to assist thee to have thy necessities and, insofar as attainable, thy other desires. It is to enable thee to realize thy most cherished desires by defending them from thy casual wishes. Like a bright light in a dark cave thy budget shows up the leaks from thy purse and enables thee to stop them and control thy expenditures for definite and gratifying purposes."

"This, then, is the second cure for a lean purse. Budget thy expenses that thou mayest have coins to pay for thy necessities, to pay for thy enjoyments, and to gratify thy worthwhile desires without spending more than nine-tenths of thy earnings."

THE THIRD CURE

Make thy gold multiply

"I tell you, my students, a man's wealth is not in the coins he carries in his purse; it is the income he buildeth, the golden stream that continually floweth into his purse and keepeth it always bulging. That is what every man desireth. That is what thou, each one of thee, desire: an income that continues to come whether thou work or travel.

"Great income I have acquired. So great that I am called very rich. My loans to responsible traders and craftsmen were my first training in profitable investment. Gaining wisdom from this experience, I extended my loans and investments as my capital increased. From a few sources at first, from many sources later, flowed into my purse a golden stream of wealth available for such wise uses as I should decide.

"Behold, from my humble earnings I had begotten a hoard of golden slaves, so to speak, each laboring and earning more gold. As they labored for me, so their children also labored and their children's children until great was the income from their combined efforts.

"This, then, is the third cure for a lean purse: to put each coin to laboring that it may reproduce its kind as the flocks of the field and help bring to thee income, a stream of wealth that shall flow constantly into thy purse."

THE FOURTH CURE

Guard thy treasures from loss

———

"Misfortune loves a shining mark. Gold in a man's purse must be guarded with firmness, else it be lost. Thus it is wise that we must first secure small amounts and learn to protect them before the gods trust us with larger.

"Every owner of gold is tempted by opportunities whereby it would seem that he could make large sums by its investment in most plausible projects. Often friends and relatives are eagerly entering such investment and urge him to follow.

"The first sound principle of investment is security for thy principal. Is it wise to be intrigued by larger earnings when thy principal may be lost? I say not. The penalty of risk is probable loss. Before parting with thy treasure, study carefully each assurance that it may be safely reclaimed. Be not misled by romantic desires to make wealth rapidly.

"Before thou loan it to any man assure thyself of his ability to repay and his reputation for doing so. Before thou entrust it as an investment in any field acquaint thyself with the dangers that may beset it."

"This, then, is the fourth cure for a lean purse, and of great importance to prevent thy purse from being emptied once it has become well filled. Guard thy treasure from loss by investing only where thy principal is safe, where it may be reclaimed if desired, and where thou will not fail to collect a fair rental. Consult with wise men. Secure the advice of those experienced in the profitable handling of gold. Let their wisdom protect thy treasure from unsafe investments."

THE FIFTH CURE

Make of thy dwelling a profitable investment

"If a man setteth aside nine parts of his earnings upon which to live and enjoy life, and if any part of this nine parts he can turn into a profitable invest-ment without detriment to his well-being, then so much faster will his treasures grow.

"All too many of our men of Babylon do raise their families in unseemly quarters where they pay to exacting landlords high rents. No man's family can fully enjoy life unless they do have a plot of ground wherein children can play in the clean earth and where the wife may raise not only blossoms but good rich herbs.

"I recommend that every man own the roof that sheltereth him and his.

"Nor is it beyond the ability of any well-intentioned man to own his home. Hath not our great king so widely extended the walls of Babylon that within them much land is now unused and may be purchased at reasonable sums?

"Also I say to you, that the moneylenders gladly consider the desires of men who seek homes for their families. Readily may thou borrow for such commendable purposes, if thou can show a reasonable portion of the necessary sum which thou thyself hath provided for the purpose.

"Then when the house be built, thou canst pay the moneylender with the same regularity as thou didst pay the landlord. Because each payment will reduce thy indebtedness to the moneylender, a few years will satisfy his loan.

"There come many blessings to the man who owneth his own house. And greatly will it reduce his cost of living, making available more of his earnings for pleasures and the gratification of his desires. This, then, is the fifth cure for a lean purse: Own thy own home."

THE SIXTH CURE
Insure a future income

"The life of every man proceedeth from his childhood to his old age. This is the path of life and no man may deviate from it unless the Gods call him prematurely to the world beyond. Therefore do I say that it behooves a man to make preparation for a suitable income in the days to come, when he is no longer young, and to make preparations for his family should he be no longer with them.

"There are diverse ways by which a man may provide safety for his future. He may provide a hiding place and there bury a secret treasure. Yet, no matter with what skill it be hidden, it may nevertheless become the loot of thieves. For this reason I recommend not this plan.

"A man may buy houses or lands for this purpose. If wisely chosen as to their usefulness and value in the future, they are permanent in their value and their earnings or sale will provide well for his purpose.

"A man may loan a small sum to the money-lender and increase it at regular periods. The rental which the moneylender adds to this will largely add to its increase. When such a small payment made with regularity doth produce such profitable results, no man can afford not to insure a treasure for his old age and the protection of his family, no matter how prosperous his business and his investments may be.

"This, then, is the sixth cure for a lean purse: provide in advance for the needs of thy growing age and the protection of thy family."

THE SEVENTH CURE
Increase thy ability to earn

"I now speak of one of the most vital remedies for a lean purse. Yet, I will talk not of gold but of yourselves, of the men beneath the robes who do sit before me. I will talk to you of those things within the minds and lives of men which do work for or against their success.

"One of the most vital requirements to increase your earnings is a strong desire to earn more, a proper and commendable desire. Preceding accomplishment must be desire. Thy desires must be strong and definite. General desires are but weak longings. For a man to wish to be rich is of little purpose. For a man to desire five pieces of gold is a tangible desire which he can press to fulfillment. After he has backed his desire for five pieces of gold with strength of purpose to secure it, next he can find similar ways to obtain ten pieces and then twenty pieces and later a thousand pieces and, behold, he has become wealthy. In learning to secure his one definite small desire, he hath trained himself to secure a larger one. This is the process by which wealth is accumulated: first in small sums, then in larger ones as a man learns and becomes more capable.

"Desires must be simple and definite. They defeat their own purpose should they be too many, too confusing, or beyond one's training to accomplish.

"As a man perfecteth himself in his calling even so doth his ability to earn increase. In those days when I was a humble scribe carving upon the clay for a few coppers each day, I observed that other workers did more than I and were paid more. Therefore, did I determine that I would be exceeded by none. Nor did it take long for me to discover the reason for their greater success. More interest in my work, more concentration upon my task, more persistence in my effort, and, behold, few men could carve more tablets in a day than I.

"The more of wisdom we know, the more we may earn. That man who seeks to learn more of his craft shall be richly rewarded. Always do the affairs of man change and improve because keen-minded men seek greater skill that they may better serve those upon whose patronage they depend. Therefore, I urge all men to be in the front rank of progress and not to stand still.

"Many things come to make a man's life rich with gainful experiences. Such things as the following a man must do if he respects himself: He must pay his debts with all the promptness within his power, not purchasing that for which he is unable to pay. He must take care of his family that they may think and speak well of him. He must make a will of record that, in case the gods call him, proper and honorable division of his property be accomplished. He must have compassion upon those who are injured and smitten by misfortune and aid them within reasonable limits. He must do deeds of thoughtfulness to those dear to him.

"Thus the seventh and last remedy for a lean purse is to cultivate thy own powers, to study and become wiser, to become more skillful, to so act as to respect thyself."

Chapter Four
Meet the Goddess of Good Luck

We all hope to be favored by the whimsical Goddess of Good Luck. Is there some way we can meet
her and attract, not only her favorable attention,
but her generous favors? Is there a way to attract
good luck?

That is just what the men of ancient Babylon
wished to know

Among the many who frequented the Temple
of Learning, was a wise rich man named Arkad,
the richest man in Babylon. He had his own special hall where almost any evening a large group
gathered to discuss and argue interesting subjects.
We now listen in to see whether they knew how to
attract good luck.

"I see no reason," Arkad announced," that the
good goddess of luck would take any interest in
any man's bet upon a horse race or at the gaming
tables. To me she is a goddess of love and dignity
whose pleasure it is to aid those who are in need
and to reward those who are deserving.

"In tilling the soil, in honest trading, in all of
man's occupations, there is opportunity to make
a profit upon his efforts and his transactions. Perhaps not all the time will he be rewarded because
sometimes his judgment may be faulty, and other

times the winds and the weather may defeat his efforts. Yet, if he persists, he may usually expect to realize his profit. This is so because the chances of profit are always in his favor.

"But when a man playeth the games, the situation is reversed for the chances of profit are always against him.

"We must seek good luck in such places as the goddess frequents. Now, suppose we consider our trades and businesses. Is it not natural if we conclude a profitable transaction to consider it not good luck but a just reward for our efforts? I am inclined to think we may be overlooking the gifts of the goddess. Perhaps she really does assist us when we do not appreciate her generosity.

"Who among you," Arkad asked, "have had good luck within your grasp only to see it escape?"

Many hands were raised.

"When sound opportunity stands before thee," the wise man continued, "it is offering a chance that may lead to wealth. I beg of thee, do not delay.

"Good luck waits to come to that man who accepts opportunity. To the building of an estate there must always be the beginning. That start may be a few pieces of gold or silver which a man diverts from his earnings to his first investment.

"To take his first start to building an estate is as good luck as can come to any man. With all men, that first step, which changes them from men who earn from their own labor to men who draw dividends from the earnings of their gold, is important. Some, fortunately, take it when young and thereby outstrip in financial success those who do take it later.

"Opportunity will not wait. She thinks if a man desires to be lucky he will step quick.

"There is much wisdom in making a payment immediately when we are convinced our bargain is wise. If the bargain be good, then dost thou need protection against thy own weaknesses as much as against any other man. We mortals are changeable. Alas, I must say more apt to change our minds when right than wrong. Wrong, we are stubborn indeed. Right, we are prone to vacillate and let opportunity escape. My first judgment is my best."

"The spirit of procrastination is within all men. We desire riches; yet, how often when opportunity doth appear before us, that spirit of procrastination from within doth urge various delays in our acceptance. In listening to it we do become our own worst enemies.

"The truth is this: Good luck can be enticed by accepting opportunity.

"Those eager to grasp opportunities for their betterment, do attract the interest of the good goddess. She is ever anxious to aid those who please her. Men of action please her best."

MEN OF ACTION ARE FAVORED
BY THE GODDESS OF GOOD LUCK

Chapter Five
The Five Laws of Gold

Gold is reserved for those who know its laws and abide by them. Hence we now reflect on the laws we have so far learned. Here are:

THE FIVE LAWS OF GOLD

1. Gold cometh gladly and in increasing quantity to any man who will put by not less than one-tenth or his earnings to create an estate for his future and that of his family.

2. Gold laboreth diligently and contentedly for the wise owner who finds for it profitable employment, multiplying even as the flocks of the field.

3. Gold clingeth to the protection of the cautious owner who invests it under the advice of men wise in its handling.

4. Gold slippeth away from the man who invests it in businesses or purposes with which he is not familiar or which are not approved by those skilled in its keep.

5. Gold flees the man who would force it to impossible earnings or who followeth the alluring advice of tricksters and schemers or who trusts it to his own inexperience and romantic desires in investment.

These are the five laws of gold. I do proclaim them as of greater value than gold itself, for they demonstrate how to continually procure its safeguard.

Chapter Six
The Gold Lender of Babylon

The gold lender of Babylon spoke as follows:

"Gold bringeth unto its possessor responsibility and a changed position with his fellow men. It bringeth fear lest he lose it or it be tricked away from him. It bringeth a feeling of power and ability to do good. Likewise, it bringeth opportunities whereby his good intentions may bring him into difficulties.

"If you desire to help thy friend, do so in a way that will not bring thy friend's burdens upon thyself.

"The safest loans, my token box tells me, are to those whose possessions are of more value than the one they desire. They own lands, or jewels, or camels, or other things which could be sold to repay the loan. Some of the tokens given to me are jewels of more value than the loan. Others are promises that if the loan be not repaid as agreed they will deliver to me certain property settlement. On loans like those I am assured that my gold will be returned with the rental thereon, for the loan is based on property.

"In another class are those who have the capacity to earn. They labor or serve and are paid. They have income and if they are honest and suffer no misfortune, I know that they also can repay the gold I loan them and the rental to which I am entitled. Such loans are based on human effort.

"Others are those who have neither property nor assured earning capacity. Life is hard and there will always be some who cannot adjust themselves to it. Alas for the loans I make them, even though they be no larger than a pence, my token box may censure me in the years to come unless they be guaranteed by good friends of the borrower who know him honorable.

"And mind you that humans in the throes of great emotions are not safe risks for the gold lender.

"Youth is ambitious. Youth would take short cuts to wealth and the desirable things for which it stands. To secure wealth quickly youth often borrows unwisely. Youth, never having had experience, cannot realize that hopeless debt is like a deep pit into which one may descend quickly and where one may struggle vainly for many days. It is a pit of sorrow and regrets where the brightness of the sun is overcast and night is made unhappy by restless sleeping. Yet, I do not discourage borrowing gold. I encourage it. I recommend it if it be for a wise purpose. I myself made my first real success as a merchant with borrowed gold.

"But be not swayed by the fantastic plans of impractical men who think they see ways to force thy gold to make earnings unusually large. Such plans are the creations of dreamers unskilled in the safe and dependable laws of trade. Be conservative in what thou expect it to earn that thou mayest keep and enjoy thy treasure. To hire it out with a promise of usurious returns is to invite loss.

"Associate with men and enterprises whose success is established that thy treasure may earn liberally under their skillful use and be guarded safely by their wisdom.

"Ere thou goest read this which I have carved beneath the lid of my token box. It applies equally to the borrower and the lender:

BETTER A LITTLE CAUTION
THAN A GREAT REGRET

Chapter Seven
The Camel Trader of Babylon

The hungrier one becomes, the clearer one's mind works—also the more sensitive one becomes to the odors of food.

Tarkad certainly thought so. For two whole days he had tasted no food except two figs purloined from over the wall of a garden. Never before had he realized how much food was brought to the markets of Babylon, and how good it smelled.

Lost in his thoughts, he found himself face to face with the one man he wished avoid, the tall bony figure of Dabasir, the camel trader. Of all the friends and others from whom he had borrowed small sums, Dabasir made him feel the most uncomfortable because of Tarkad's failure to repay promptly.

Upon meeting his gaze, Tarkad stuttered and his face flushed. He had naught in his empty stomach to nerve him to argue with Dabasir. "I am sorry, very sorry," he said, "but this day I have neither the copper nor the silver with which I could repay."

"Then get it," Dabasir said. "Surely thou canst get hold of a few coppers and a piece of silver to repay the generosity of an old friend of thy father who aided thee whenst thou wast in need?"

"'Tis because ill fortune does pursue me that I cannot pay."

"Ill fortune! Wouldst blame the gods for thine own weakness? Ill fortune pursues every man who thinks more of borrowing than of repaying. Come with me, boy, while I eat. I am hungry and I would tell thee a tale."

Settling down in the eating house, Dabasir began. "When I was a young man I learned the trade of my father, the making of saddles. I worked with him in his shop and took to myself a wife. Being young and not greatly skilled, I could earn but little, just enough to support my excellent wife in a modest way. I craved good things which I could not afford. Soon I found that the shopkeepers would trust me to pay later even though I could not pay at the time.

"Being young and without experience I did not know that he who spends more than he earns is sowing the winds of needless self-indulgence from which he is sure to reap whirlwinds of trouble and humiliation. So I indulged my whims for fine raiment and bought luxuries for my good wife and our home, beyond our means.

"I paid as I could and for a while all went well. But in time I discovered I could not use my earnings both to live upon and to pay my debts. Creditors began to pursue me to pay for my extravagant purchases and life became miserable. I borrowed from my friends, but could not repay them either. Things went from bad to worse. My wife returned to her father and I decided to leave Babylon and seek another city where a young man might have better chances.

"For two years I had a restless and unsuccessful life working for caravan traders. From this I fell in with a set of likable robbers who scoured the desert for unarmed caravans. Such deeds were unworthy of the son of my father, but I was seeing the world through a colored stone and did not realize to what degradation I had fallen.

"One day our leaders were killed, and the rest of us were taken to Damascus where we were stripped of our clothing and sold as slaves.

In bondage I one day told my story to the wife of my new master. Rather than express pity, she replied: "'How can you call yourself a free man when your weakness has brought you to this? If a man has in himself the soul of a slave will he not become one no matter what his birth, even as water seeks its level? If a man has within him the soul of a free man, will he not become respected and honored in has own city in spite of his misfortune?

"'Have you a desire to repay the just debts you owe in Babylon?' she asked.

"Yes, I have the desire, but I see no way," I said.

"'If thou contentedly let the years slip by and make no effort to repay, then thou hast but the contemptible soul of a slave. No man is otherwise who cannot respect himself, and no man can respect himself who does not repay honest debts.'

"But what can I do who am a slave in Syria?

"'Stay a slave in Syria, thou weakling.'

"I am not a weakling," I said.

"'Then prove it.'

"How?"

"'Does not thy great king fight his enemies in every way he can and with every force he has? Thy debts are thy enemies. They ran thee out of Babylon. You left them alone and they grew too strong for thee. Hadst fought them as a man, thou couldst have conquered them and been one honored among the townspeople. But thou had not the soul to fight them and behold thy pride hast gone down until thou are a slave in Syria.'

"Much I thought over her accusations and many defensive phrases I worded to prove myself not a slave at heart, but I was not to have the chance to use them. Three days later she came to me and said: 'Saddle the two best camels in my husband's herd. Tie on water skins and saddlebags for a long journey.'

"Deep in the desert she asked me: 'Dabasir, hast thou the soul of a free man or the soul of a slave?'

"The soul of a free man," I said.

"'Now is thy chance to prove it. 'Take these camels'—she gestured at part of the herd—'and make thy escape.'

"I needed no further urging, but thanked her and was away into the night."

"Day after day I plodded along. Food and water gave out. The heat of the sun was merciless. At the end of the ninth day, I slid from the back of my mount with the feeling that I was too weak to ever remount and I would surely die.

"I looked across into the barren distance and once again came to me the question, 'Have I the soul of a slave or the soul of a free man?' Then I realized that if I had the soul of a slave, I should give up, lie down in the desert and die.

"But if I had the soul of a free man, what then? Surely I would force my way back to Babylon, repay the people who had trusted me, bring happiness to my wife who truly loved me and bring peace and contentment to my parents.

"'Thy debts are thine enemies who have run thee out of Babylon,' the master's wife had said. Yes it was so. Why had I refused to stand my ground like a man?

"Then a strange thing happened. All the world seemed to be of a different color. At last I saw the true values in life.

"Die in the desert! Not I! With a new vision, I saw the things that I must do. First I would go back to Babylon and face every man to whom I owed an unpaid debt. I should tell them that after years of wandering and misfortune, I had come back to pay my debts as fast as the Gods would permit. Next I should make a home for my wife and become a citizen of whom my parents should be proud.

"I staggered to my feet. What mattered hunger? What mattered thirst? They were but incidents on the road to Babylon. Within me surged the soul of a free man going back to conquer his enemies and reward his friends. I thrilled with the great resolve.

"We found water. We passed into a more fertile country where were grass and fruit. We found the trail to Babylon because the soul of a free man looks at life as a series of problems to be solved and solves them, while the soul of a slave whines, 'What can I do who am but a slave?'

"How about thee, Tarkad? Dost thy empty stomach make thy head exceedingly clear? Art thou ready to take the road that leads back to self-respect? Canst thou see the world in its true color? Hast thou the desire to pay thy debts, however many they may be, and once again be a man respected in Babylon?"

Moisture came to the eyes of the youth. He rose eagerly to his knees. "Thou has shown me a vision; already I feel the soul of a free man surge within me."

"Where the determination is, the way can be found," Dabasir said, returning to his tale. "I now had the determination so I set out to find a way. First I visited every man to whom I was indebted and begged his indulgence until I could earn that with which to repay. Most of them met me gladly. Several reviled me but others offered to help me; one indeed did give me the very help I needed.

"Gradually I was able to repay every copper and every piece of silver. Then at last I could hold up my head and feel that I was an honorable man among men."

So ended the tale of Dabasir the camel trader of old Babylon. He found his own soul when he realized a great truth, a truth that had been known by wise men long before his time. It has led men of all ages out of difficulties and into success, and it will continue to do so for those who have the wisdom to understand its magic power. It is for any man to use who reads these lines:

WHERE THE DETERMINATION IS,
THE WAY CAN BE FOUND

Chapter Eight
The Luckiest Man in Babylon

At the head of his caravan, proudly rode Sharru Nada, the merchant prince of Babylon. He liked fine cloth and wore rich and becoming robes. He liked fine animals and sat easily upon his Arabian stallion. To look at him one would hardly have guessed his secret: years earlier he had been a slave in the city that now counted him among its wealthiest citizens.

His young journeyman, Hadan Gula, broke in upon his thoughts, "Why dost thou work so hard, riding always with thy caravan upon its long journeys? If I had wealth equal to thine, I would live like a prince. Never across the hot desert would I ride. I would spend the shekels as fast as they came to my purse. That would be a life to my liking, a life worth living."

"Wouldst thou leave no time for work?" the older man asked.

"Work was made for slaves," Hadan Gula said.

"Did not thy grandfather tell thee I was once a slave?"

"He often spoke of thee but never hinted of this."

"Any man may find himself a slave. It was a gaming house and barley beer that brought me disaster."

"But tell me," Hadan Gula asked, "how didst thou regain freedom?"

Sharru Nada remembered back to his youth. "The first night I was in the slave encampment waiting to be sold the next morning, terror gripped me. I could not sleep. I crowded close to the guard rope, and when the others slept, I attracted the attention of Godoso who was doing the first guard watch.

"'Tell me, Godoso,' I whispered, 'when we get to Babylon will we be sold to the walls?' The task of building the city walls was brutal and a near-certain death sentence.

"'Why you want to know?' he asked.

"'Canst thou not understand?' I said. 'I am young. I want to live. I don't want to be worked or beaten to death on the walls. Is there any chance for me to get a good master?'

"He whispered back, 'I tell you something. Thou good fellow, give me no trouble. Most times we go first to slave market. Listen now. When the buyers come, tell 'em you a good worker, like to work hard for good master. Make 'em want to buy. You not make 'em buy, next day you carry brick. Mighty hard work.'

"After he walked away, I lay in the warm sand, looking up at the stars and thinking about work. Another slave, a wise one named Megiddo, told me that work was his best friend. It made me wonder if it would be my best friend. Certainly it would be if it helped me out of this.

"The following morning, Meggido talked to me earnestly to impress upon me how valuable work would be to me in the future: 'Some men hate it. They make it their enemy. Better to treat it like a friend, make thyself like it. Don't mind because it is hard. If thou thinkest about what a good house thou build, then who cares if the beams are heavy and it is far from the well to carry the water for the plaster. Promise me, boy, if thou get a master, work for him as hard as thou canst. If he does not appreciate all thou do, never mind. Remember, work, well done, does good to the man who does it. It makes him a better man.'

"He stopped as a burly farmer came to the enclosure and looked at us critically. Megiddo asked about his farm and crops, soon convincing him that he would be a valuable man. After violent bargaining with the slave dealer, the farmer drew a fat purse from beneath his robe, and soon Megiddo had followed his new master out of sight.

"A few other men were sold during the morning. At noon Godoso confided to me that the dealer was disgusted and would not stay over another night but would take all who remained at sundown to the king's buyer and put them to work on the walls. I was becoming desperate when a fat, good-natured man walked up to the pen and inquired if there was a baker among us.

"I approached him saying, 'Why should a good baker like thyself seek another baker of inferior ways? Would it not be easier to teach a willing man like myself thy skilled ways? Look at me, I am young, strong, and like to work. Give me a chance and I will do my best to earn gold and silver for thy purse.'

"He was impressed by my willingness and began bargaining with the dealer. At last, much to my joy, the deal was closed. I followed my new master away, thinking I was the luckiest man in Babylon.

"My new home was much to my liking. Nana-naid, my master, taught me how to grind the barley in the stone bowl that stood in the courtyard, how to build the fire in the oven, and then how to grind very fine the sesame flour for the honey cakes. I had a couch in the shed where his grain was stored. The old slave housekeeper, Swasti, fed me well and was pleased at how I helped her with the heavy tasks.

"Here was the chance I had longed for to make myself valuable to my master and, I hoped, to find a way to earn my freedom. I asked Nana-naid to show me how to knead the bread and to bake. This he did, much pleased at my willingness. Later, when I could do this well, I asked him to show me how to make the honey cakes, and soon I was doing all the baking. My master was glad to be idle, but Swasti shook her head in disapproval. 'No work to do is bad for any man,' she declared.

"I felt it was time for me to think of a way by which I might start to earn coins to buy my freedom. As the baking was finished at noon, I thought Nana-naid would approve if I found profitable employment for the afternoons and might share my earnings with me. Then the thought came to me, why not bake more of the honey cakes and peddle them to hungry men upon the streets of the city?

"When I told him of my plan to peddle our honey cakes, he was well pleased. 'Here is what we will do,' he suggested. 'Thou sellest them at two for a penny, then half of the pennies will be mine to pay for the flour and the honey and the wood to bake them. Of the rest, I shall take half and thou shall keep half.'

"I was much pleased by his generous offer that I might keep for myself one-fourth of my sales. I worked day and night and my success at selling my honey cakes grew. My master was pleased. And as the months passed I continued to add pennies to my purse. It began to have a comforting weight upon my belt. Work was proving to be my best friend, just as Megiddo had said.

"I was happy but Swasti was worried. 'Thy master, I fear to have him spend so much time at the gaming houses,' she said.

"As I went forth with my tray of cakes every day, I soon found regular customers. One of these was none other than your grandfather, Arad Gula. He was a rug merchant and sold to the housewives, going from one end of the city to the other, accompanied by a donkey loaded high with rugs. He would buy two cakes for himself and two for his slave, always tarrying to talk with me while they ate them.

"Thy grandfather said something to me one day that I shall always remember. 'I like thy cakes, boy, but better still I like the fine enterprise with which thou offerest them. Such spirit can carry thee far on the road to success.' But how canst thou understand, Hadan Gula, what such words of encouragement could mean to a slave boy, lonesome in a great city, struggling with all he had in him to find a way out of his humiliation?

"One day in the markets Arad Gula asked me, 'Why dost thou work so hard?' Almost the same question thou asked of me today, dost thou remember? I told him what Megiddo had said about work and how it was proving to be my best friend. I showed him with pride my wallet of pennies and explained how I was saving them to buy my freedom.

"'When thou art free, what wilt thou do?' he asked.

"'I intend to become a merchant,' I said.

"At that, he confided in me. Something I had never suspected. 'Thou knowest not that I, also, am a slave. I am in partnership with my master.'

"After confiding that he was a slave," Sharru Nada continued, 'he explained how anxious he had been to earn his freedom. Now that he had enough money to buy this he was much disturbed as to what he should do. He was no longer making good sales and feared to leave the support of his master.

"I protested his indecision: 'Cling no longer to thy master. Get once again the feeling of being a free man. Act like a free man and succeed like one! Decide what thou desirest to accomplish and then work will aid thee to achieve it!' He went on his way saying he was glad I had shamed him for his cowardice.

"Back home I earned that Swasti's fears were well-founded. The master's loses had been mounting, and I discovered that he had put me up as collateral. While I was doing the baking next morning, the moneylender came with a man he called Sasi. This man looked me over and said I would do.

"The moneylender waited not for my master to return. With only the robe on my back and the purse of pennies hanging safely from my belt, I was hurried away.

"I was whirled away from my dearest hopes as the hurricane snatches the tree from the forest and casts it into the surging sea. Again a gaming house and barley beer had caused me disaster.

"Sasi was a blunt, gruff man. As he led me across the city, I told him of the good work I had been doing for Nana-naid and said I hoped to do good work for him. He offered no encouragement: he told me I was bound for the walls.

"The walls were all that I had heard. Picture a desert with not a tree, just low shrubs and a sun burning with such fury the water in our barrels became so hot we could scarcely drink it. Then picture rows of men, going down into the deep excavation and lugging heavy baskets of dirt up soft, dusty trails from daylight until dark. Picture food served in open troughs from which we helped ourselves like swine. We had no tents, no straw for beds. That was the situation in which I found myself. I buried my wallet in a marked spot, wondering if I would ever dig it up again.

"At first I worked with good will, but as the months dragged on, I felt my spirit breaking. Then the heat fever took hold of my weary body. I lost my appetite and could scarcely eat. At night I would toss in unhappy wakefulness. Yet I was just as willing to work as Megiddo; he could not have worked harder than I. Why did not my work bring me happiness and success? Was I to work the rest of my life without gaining my desires? All of these questions were jumbled in my mind and I had not an answer. Indeed, I was sorely confused.

"Several days later when it seemed that I was at the end of my endurance and with my questions still unanswered, Sasi sent for me. A messenger had come from my master to take me back to Babylon. I dug up my precious wallet, wrapped myself in the tattered remnants of my robe and was on my way.

"When we rode to the courtyard of my master's house, imagine my surprise when I saw Arad Gula awaiting me. He helped me down and hugged me like a long lost brother.

"As we went our way I would have followed him as a slave should follow his master, but he would not permit me. He put his arm about me, saying, 'I hunted everywhere for thee: When I had almost given up hope, I did meet Swasti who told me of the moneylender, who directed me to thy noble owner. A hard bargain he did drive and made me pay an outrageous price, but thou art worth it. Thy philosophy and thy enterprise have been my inspiration to this new success. We are going to Damascus and I need thee for my partner. In one moment thou will be a free man!'

"Tears of gratitude filled my eyes. 1 knew I was the luckiest man in Babylon. In the time of my greatest distress, work didst indeed prove my best friend. My willingness to work enabled me to escape being sold to slave gangs upon the walls. It also so impressed thy grandfather, he selected me for his partner.

"Life is rich with many pleasures for men to enjoy," Sharru Nada concluded to his young friend. "Each has its place. I am glad that work is not reserved for slaves. Were that the case I would be deprived of my greatest pleasure. Many things do I enjoy, but nothing takes the place of work."

Chapter Nine
The Clay Tablets of Babylon

Alfred H. Shrewsbury, a young archeologist at Nottingham University, was breathless with excitement at the five clay tablets that had just arrived from excavation in the ruins of Babylon.

He wrote to the excavator: "You will be as astonished at the story they relate. One expects the dim and distant past to speak of romance and adventure. When instead it discloses the problem of a person named Dabasir to pay off his debts, one realizes that conditions upon this old world have not changed as much in five thousand years as one might expect.

"It's odd, you know, but these old inscriptions rather 'rag' me. Being a college professor, I am supposed to be a thinking human being possessing a working knowledge of most subjects. Yet, here comes this old chap out of the ruins of Babylon to offer a way I had never heard of to pay off my debts and at the same time acquire gold to jingle in my wallet. Pleasant thought, I say, and interesting to prove whether it will work as well nowadays as it did in Babylon. Mrs. Shrewsbury and myself are planning to try out his plan upon our own affairs, which could be much improved."

His translations went as follows:

TABLET ONE

Now, when the moon becometh full, I, Dabasir, who am but recently returned from slavery in Syria, with the determination to pay my many debts and become a man of means worthy of respect in my native city of Babylon, do here engrave upon the clay a permanent record of my affairs to guide and assist me in carrying through my high desires.

This plan includeth three purposes which are my hope and desire.

First, the plan doth provide for my future prosperity. Therefore one-tenth of all I earn shall be set aside as my own to keep.

Second, I shall support and clothe my good wife who hath returned to me with loyalty from the house of her father. To take good care of a faithful wife putteth self-respect into the heart of a man and addeth strength and determination to his purposes.

Therefore seven-tenths of all I earn shall be used to provide a home, clothes to wear, and food to eat, with a bit extra to spend, that our lives be not lacking in pleasure and enjoyment. But he doth further enjoin the greatest care that we spend not greater than seven-tenths of what I earn for these worthy purposes. Herein lieth the success of the plan. I must live upon this portion and never use more nor buy what I may not pay for out of this portion.

TABLET TWO

Third, the plan doth provide that out of my earnings my debts shall be paid. Therefore each time the moon is full, two-tenths of all I have earned shall be divided honorably and fairly among those who have trusted me and to whom I am indebted. Thus in due time will all my indebtedness be surely paid.

Here the professor jotted on his notepad: "Paying debt surpasses savings. One-tenth to savings; two-tenths to debt; seven-tenths to home and family."

TABLET THREE

Now that I realize how I can repay my debts in small sums of my earnings, do I realize the great extent of my folly in running away from the results of my extravagances.

Therefore have I visited my creditors and explained to them that I have no resources with which to pay except my ability to earn, and that I intend to apply two-tenths of all I earn upon my indebtedness evenly and honestly. This much can I pay but no more. Therefore if they be patient, in time my obligations will be paid in full.

Ahmar, whom I thought my best friend, re-viled me bitterly and I left him in humiliation. Birejik, the farmer, pleaded that I pay him first as he didst badly need help. Alkahad, the house owner, was indeed disagreeable and insisted that he would make me trouble unless I didst soon settle in full with him.

All the rest willingly accepted my proposal. Therefore am I more determined than ever to carry through, being convinced that it is easier to pay one's debts than to avoid them.

TABLET FOUR

Thus I have divided according to the plan. One-tenth have I set aside to keep as my own, seven-tenths have I divided with my good wife to pay for our living.

Two-tenths have I divided among my credi-tors as evenly as could be done in coppers.

I did not see Ahmar but left it with his wife. Birejik was so pleased he would kiss my hand. Old Alkahad alone was grouchy and said I must pay faster. To which I replied that if I were per-mitted to be well fed and not worried, that alone would enable me to pay faster. All the others thanked me and spoke well of my efforts.

Therefore, at the end of one moon, my indebtedness is reduced by almost four pieces of silver and I possess almost two pieces of silver besides, upon which no man hath claim. My heart is lighter than it hath been for a long time.

TABLET FIVE

Again the moon shines full and I remember that it is long since I carved upon the clay. Twelve moons in truth have come and gone. But this day I will not neglect my record because upon this day I have paid the last of my debts. This is the day upon which my good wife and my thankful self celebrate with great feasting that our determination hath been achieved.

My wife looketh upon me with a light in her eyes that doth make a man have confidence in himself. Yet it is the plan that hath made my success. I do commend it to all who wish to get ahead. For truly if it will enable an ex-slave to pay his debts and have gold in his purse, will it not aid any man to find independence? Nor am I finished with it, for I am convinced that if I follow it further it will make me rich among men.

After completing his translation, Shrewsbury wrote again to his friend: "You will possibly remember my writing a year ago that Mrs. Shrewsbury and myself intended to try his plan for getting out of debt and at the same time having gold to jingle. You may have guessed, even though we tried to keep it from our friends, our desperate straits.

"We were frightfully humiliated for years by a lot of old debts and worried sick for fear some of the tradespeople might start a scandal that would force me out of the college. We paid and paid—every shilling we could squeeze out of income—but it was hardly enough to hold things even. Besides we were forced to do all our buying where we could get further credit regardless of higher costs.

"It developed into one of those vicious circles that grow worse instead of better. Our struggles were getting hopeless. We could not move to less costly rooms because we owed the landlord. There did not appear to be anything we could do to improve our situation.

"Then comes the old camel trader from Babylon, with a plan to do just what we wished to accomplish. He jolly well stirred us up to follow his system. We made a list of all our debts and I took it around and showed it to every one we owed. I explained how it was simply impossible for me to ever pay them the way things were going along. They could readily see this themselves from the figures. Then I explained that the only way I saw to pay in full was to set aside twenty percent of my income each month to be divided pro rata, which would pay them in full in a little over two years.

Then, in the meantime, we would go on a cash basis and give them the further benefit of our cash purchases.

"They were really quite decent. Our greengrocer, a wise old chap, put it in a way that helped to bring around the rest. 'If you pay for all you buy and then pay some of what you owe, that is better than you have done.'

"Then we began scheming on how to live upon seventy percent. We were determined to keep that extra ten percent to jingle. It was like having an adventure to make the change. We enjoyed figuring this way and that to live comfortably upon that remaining seventy-percent. We started with rent and managed to secure a fair reduction. Next we put our favorite brands of tea and such under suspicion and were agreeably surprised how often we could purchase superior qualities at less cost.

"We managed and right cheerfully at that. What a relief it proved to have our affairs in such a shape we were no longer persecuted by past due accounts.

"I must not neglect, however, to tell you about that extra ten percent we were supposed to jingle. Well, we did jingle it for some time. Now don't laugh too soon. You see, that is the sporty part. It is the real fun to start accumulating money that you do not want to spend. There is more pleasure in running up such a surplus than there could be in spending it.

"After we had jingled to our hearts' content, we found a more profitable use for it. We took up an investment upon which we could pay that ten percent each month. This is proving to be the most satisfying part of our regeneration. It is the first thing we pay out of my check.

"There is a most gratifying sense of security to know our investment is growing steadily. By the time my teaching days are over it should be a snug sum, large enough so the income will take care of us from then on.

"All this out of my same old check. Difficult to believe, yet absolutely true.

"At the end of the next year, when all our old bills shall have been paid, we will have more to pay upon our investment besides some extra for travel. We are determined never again to permit our living expenses to exceed seventy percent of our income.

"The chap who carved these tablets had a timeless message, a message so important that after five thousand years it has risen out of the ruins of Babylon, just as true and just as vital as the day it was buried."

About the Authors

Born in Missouri in 1874, **George S. Clason** attended the University of Nebraska and served in the U.S. Army during the Spanish-American War. Soon after the war he founded the Clason Map Company of Denver, Colorado, where he published the first road atlas of the U.S. and Canada. In 1926, Clason began issuing a series of pamphlets on personal financial management using fictionalized parables set in ancient Babylon. His pamphlets were first distributed free to clients by banks and insurance companies, and in 1930 Clason collected and published them in book form, where they became famous as *The Richest Man in Babylon*. Clason died in Napa, California, in 1957.

Mitch Horowitz is the PEN Award-winning author of books including *Occult America* and *The Miracle Club*. A writer-in-residence at the New York Public Library and lecturer-in-residence at the University of Philosophical Research in Los Angeles, Mitch introduces and edits G&D Media's line of Condensed Classics and is the author of the Napoleon Hill Success Course series, including *The Miracle of a Definite Chief Aim*, *The Power of the Master Mind*, and *Secrets of Self-Mastery*. His G&D titles include *The Miracle Habits* and *The Miracle Month*.

Twitter: @MitchHorowitz

Instagram: @MitchHorowitz23

CPSIA information can be obtained
at www.ICGtesting.com
Printed in the USA
JSHW020240010221
11405JS00001B/2